LETTER
TO A
CHRISTIAN

LETTER
TO A
CHRISTIAN

AUSTINE

iUniverse, Inc.
Bloomington

iUniverse books may be ordered through booksellers or by contacting:

iUniverse
1663 Liberty Drive
Bloomington, IN 47403
www.iuniverse.com
1-800-Authors (1-800-288-4677)

Because of the dynamic nature of the Internet, any Web addresses or
links contained in this book may have changed since publication and
may no longer be valid. The views expressed in this work are solely those
of the author and do not necessarily reflect the views of the publisher,
and the publisher hereby disclaims any responsibility for them.

Any people depicted in stock imagery provided by Thinkstock are models,
and such images are being used for illustrative purposes only.

Certain stock imagery © Thinkstock.

ISBN: 978-1-4502-7550-7 (pbk)
ISBN: 978-1-4502-7551-4 (cloth)
ISBN: 978-1-4502-7552-1 (ebk)

Library of Congress Control Number: 2010917727

Printed in the United States of America

iUniverse rev. date: 2/9/2011

For the body

Preface

Then Jesus said:

'When the Son of Man comes in his glory, and all the angels with him, he will sit on his throne in heavenly glory. All the nations will be gathered before him, and he will separate the people one from another as a shepherd separates the sheep from the goats. He will put the sheep on his right and the goats on his left.'

Then the King will say to those on his right,

'Come, you who are blessed by my Father; take your inheritance, the kingdom prepared for you since the creation of the world. For I was hungry and you gave me something to eat, I was thirsty and you gave me something to drink, I was a stranger and you invited me in, I needed clothes and you clothed me, I was sick and you looked after me, I was in prison and you came to visit me.'

Then the righteous will answer him,

'Lord, when did we see you hungry and feed you, or thirsty and give you something to drink? When did we see you a stranger and invite you in, or needing clothes and clothe you? When did we see you sick or in prison and go to visit you?'

The King will reply,

'I tell you the truth, whatever you did for one of the least of these brothers of mine, you did for me.'

Then he will say to those on his left,

'Depart from me, you who are cursed, into the eternal fire prepared for the devil and his angels. For I was hungry and you gave me nothing to eat, I was thirsty and you gave me nothing to drink, I was a stranger and you did not invite me in, I needed clothes and you did not clothe me, I was sick and in prison and you did not look after me.'

They also will answer,

'Lord, when did we see you hungry or thirsty or a stranger or needing clothes or sick or in prison, and did not help you?'

H e will reply,

'I tell you the truth, whatever you did not do for one of the least of these, you did not do for me.'

T hen they will go away to eternal punishment, but the righteous to eternal life."

MATTHEW 25:36-46

LETTER TO A CHRISTIAN

The church of Jesus Christ has left its first love.

Torn apart by disagreements and arguments, we are hated, but not for Christ's sake. Instead, too often we are despised for our self-righteousness and mocked for our hypocrisy.

Distracted by popular, trendy doctrines masquerading as the revolutionary good news of Jesus Christ we are irrelevant as salt and light. Our churches preach a gospel that soothes but brings no conviction. Filling the pews with tares, we sell the gospel as a self-improvement panacea that requires nothing of the hearer.

We should not be surprised then that so many Christians are immature and easily swayed by the false brilliance of the world. So focused on grasping some imagined earthly success, we prefer enslavement to the world to liberty in Christ.

Ineffective against our own sin, we are certainly unable to mount an effective opposition to Satan's deceptions in the world around us.

We fall publicly and often. Yet even as we wag our finger to scold the unsaved, we hear no outcry for our own repentance.

We've forgotten, or perhaps no longer care, that we are called out to be a *"peculiar people"* (I Peter 2:9 KJV). Humility and holiness are as foreign to us as to the rest of the world, and yet we wonder why there is no revival.

*   *   *

Almost every day since the United States went to war after 9/11, we have heard seemingly endless reports of suicide bombers attacking schools and markets, killing innocent bystanders.

Here in the West, we're stunned at the callous disregard for human life, and rightfully so. We express our disgust for these misguided suicide bombers who are willing to kill others and themselves in the name of jihad.

Yet for the believer, for those of us who are Christians, there is an irony here that we cannot overlook.

Remove the senseless murder from the equation and we're confronted with exactly the same kind of life-and-death, all-or-nothing, commitment that is expected from every believer.

Jesus Christ said:

> "Whoever has my commands and obeys them, he is the one who loves me ... If anyone loves me, he will obey my teaching ... He who does not love me will not obey my teaching."

> JOHN 14:21; 23-24 NIV

*　　*　　*

But too many of us want the best of both worlds.

We want the eternal benefits of being saved without the earthly sacrifice. So we go to church on Sunday, and then return to our "real" lives on Monday.

Regrettably, because we have been so prosperous, at least here in the West, we have become comfortable. We actually believe that we're getting away with this double-minded, half-hearted approach to following Christ, ignoring or choosing not to understand that there will be a price to pay for our laziness and slothfulness.

We ignore the explicit warnings in Scripture at our own peril.

> Be not deceived; God is not mocked: for whatsoever a man soweth, that shall he also reap.
>
> GALATIANS 6:7 KJV

> Not everyone who says to Me, Lord, Lord, will enter the kingdom of heaven, but he who does the will of My Father who is in heaven. Many will say to Me on that day, Lord, Lord, have we not prophesied in Your name and driven out demons in Your name and done many mighty works in Your name? Then I will say to them openly (publicly), I never

knew you; depart from Me, you who act wickedly.

Because you are lukewarm and neither cold nor hot, I will spew you out of My mouth! For you say, I am rich; I have prospered and grown wealthy, and I am in need of nothing; and you do not realize and understand that you are wretched, pitiable, poor, blind, and naked.

It's impossible to make this any clearer.

True salvation [true repentance] equals love for Christ.

Love for Christ equals obedience.

Jesus already said that if this is too much for us, then we don't know Him, and He will not know us.

If attendance, congregational satisfaction and dollars raised are indicators of success, then the church of Jesus Christ is more successful than ever.

We have new buildings, new auditoriums, new church compounds and complexes.

We buy sports arenas and convert them into stadium-sized churches.

We have numerous Christian titles on the *New York Times* bestseller list and just as many Christian artists on the music charts.

Evangelical Christians are as politically active today as at any time in our nation's history.

It should be brutally obvious, though, that none of this has brought revival. Instead if we're honest, we can acknowledge that too often, the church of Jesus Christ has simply exchanged the truth of God and His Word for the metrics of the world.

We have discarded the Great Commission for political activism and a self-righteous morality, substituting vocal, political opposition to cultural issues like abortion or gay marriage for the actual practice of Christianity. Our futile attempts to hold the world accountable to standards which we ourselves do not meet has exposed our own sin and left us vulnerable to valid accusations of hypocrisy.

Jesus spoke plainly when He said:

> "Hypocrites! Well did Isaiah prophesy about you, saying: 'These people draw near to me with their mouth, and honor Me with their lips, But their heart is far from me.'"

MATTHEW 15:7-9

We have become the church of weak minds, weak wills and even weaker faith—content to live our lives as close to the world as possible.

The most heartbreaking result is that we are rarely associated with either the love, the compassion or the good news of Christ. Instead, distracted by *psychobabble, prosperity* and *politics*, too many of our churches have fallen into the trap of offering a one-dimensional gospel designed to fill pews.

*   *   *

Go to a church on Main Street.

In this church, it's fashionable to talk about self-improvement and self-help. Whether fitness or finance, sermons and bestsellers alike encourage believers to fix themselves. You can hear the transforming work of Jesus Christ reduced to mindless psychobabble, through which the Christian life morphs into a never-ending process of psychoanalysis and self-soothing.

Focused almost exclusively on God's love and God's grace—ignoring God's expectation of holiness—we encourage believers, many of whom are already *thorny ground*, to wrap themselves in the doctrine of self-analysis and self-correction. We substitute the religion of self for the practice of the presence of God.

Now do not deliberately misunderstand.

Not all of us come to Christ and receive instant relief from these internal struggles.

Unfortunately, though, the attentions and energies of an overwhelming number of churches today have been completely absorbed by this "Gospel of Me." It was almost fifty years ago, when C. S. Lewis warned us of the dangers of this tendency and called it what it is: "the concentration upon self which is the mark of Hell."

It is time for the church to forsake this immature gospel that places little to no emphasis on the sacrificial nature of salvation, either in regard to the suffering of Christ on the cross or in our own lives.

We must realize that this self-absorption leads to a self-perpetuating cycle of immaturity and uselessness in the kingdom of God.

A church without spot or wrinkle cannot be rooted very firmly in the pursuit of personal well-being. It must be rooted and grounded in Christ.

*   *   *

Yet for every church on Main Street that manages to avoid getting lost in the hall of mirrors of *psychobabble*, there are too many on First Street chasing the mirage of prosperity.

We know from the book of Acts that the early church walked in such a powerful anointing of boldness and faith that unbelievers were forced to admit the reality of Christ.

Perhaps one of the reasons for their boldness was their willingness to rely on God for even their most basic needs. Quite simply, they took Christ at His word when He told them to *"lay up for yourselves treasures in heaven, where neither moth nor rust destroys and where thieves do not break in and steal"* (Matthew 6:20).

Today, we have either forgotten or we ignore the sacrificial example of Christ and the early church. Snatching every opportunity to live well themselves, pastors teach their flocks that all they need is just a little more—a little more faith to be blessed, a little more faith to be healed, or a little more faith for a new house or a new car.

Certainly, if anyone was going to be blessed with material possessions, it would have been Simon Peter, or John or Paul. After all, these disciples and many of the earliest believers quite literally left everything they had to physically follow Christ.

However, we know from history that none of these men were rewarded here on earth for their obedience. In fact, many of the apostles and earliest disciples died a martyr's death.

Did they regret their sacrifice?

Paul did not. Neither did Peter.

> Blessed be the God and Father of our Lord Jesus Christ, who according to His abundant mercy has begotten us again to a living hope through the resurrection of Jesus Christ from the dead, to an inheritance incorruptible and undefiled and that does not fade away, reserved in heaven for you.
>
> I PETER 1:3-4

Both of them understood that there is nothing to be achieved here on earth that will last or that can even begin to compare with the heavenly promises of God.

No, following Christ doesn't necessarily mean swearing a vow of poverty.

Scripture is perfectly clear that it is the love of money—not money itself—that is the root of all evil. And yes, Scripture teaches us that God is a good Father, and that we should expect good things from God. However, at no point, or at least not without taking a few verses out of context, can we imagine that prosperity—or even physical health—is the primary aim of God's transforming work in our lives.

Know this, fellow believers, the world glitters for a reason.

Satan knows that there is no better way to make sure that we forget that we are heirs with Christ than to let us get just a little taste of the good life down here. No easier way to make us forget that the faithful will rule and reign with Christ throughout eternity than to offer us a little earthly success. The demonic antagonist in C.S. Lewis'

Screwtape Letters puts it this way: "We want a whole race perpetually in pursuit of the rainbow's end."

So, if you define being *blessed* as having the peace of God which passes all understanding, the joy of the Holy Spirit which is our strength, and the redeeming love of Christ, you're absolutely right: God *has* promised you great blessing and an abundant life.

But if your definition of prosperity focuses on the things that this world has to offer, then you must see that you have been distracted by the glitter of this world.

*　　*　　*

But for the rest of the church that has not been led astray by *psychobabble* or *prosperity*, there remains *politics*.

*　　*　　*

Today, too many non-Christians believe that the church is *"primarily motivated by a political agenda and [to] promote right-wing politics."*

This is our own fault.

We have embraced causes and movements to the point that evangelical no longer means *one who shares Christ*. Instead, it means someone who is aligned with a particular political perspective—the more conservative or Republican the better.

So we vote. We march. We sign petitions. Not just as a fulfillment of our civic responsibility, but as some misguided means to bring about the change that only revival can bring.

This is just another trap.

Exchanging spiritual significance for political power has led to the basest kinds of hypocrisy and compromise within the church.

We lie down with anyone so long as they claim to be pro-life and anti-gay marriage. We compromise with people who do the very things we say that we are against, solely to obtain political results. Consequently, in our minds and unfortunately, in the minds of the world, the terms Christian and Republican have become virtually indistinguishable.

*　　*　　*

I am not saying that there is no room for Christians in politics. However, I am saying quite firmly that there is absolutely no room for politics in Christianity. We should be familiar enough with the early history of our faith to understand the inevitable results of marrying the teachings of Christ with the tools of the world.

For those who think that politics is our primary or even secondary means to be salt and light, Paul's letter to the Ephesians reminds us that

> We wrestle not against flesh and blood, but against principalities, against powers, against the rulers of the darkness of this world, against spiritual wickedness in high places.

EPHESIANS 6:12 KJV

Yet we have forsaken our spiritual weapons to engage in a physical battle against Satan's world system.

Is it any wonder then that we are losing?

We must regain a proper Biblical perspective.

First, we must remember that God uses people, leaders, and nations only for as long as he sees fit. This includes the United States.

Second, know that transformation and revival can come, but not because the right or wrong person is elected president or nominated to the Supreme Court. Voting, marching, signing petitions and lobbying will not advance the cause of Christ.

Revival and transformation will come if, and only if, we begin to take God and His word seriously. God tells us

> "If My people who are called by My
> name will humble themselves, and
> pray and seek My face, and turn
> from their wicked ways, then I will
> hear from heaven, and will forgive
> their sin and heal their land."

II Chronicles 7:14

Read this very carefully. God is speaking in the Old Testament to His people. He says that *we* must humble *ourselves* and seek His face. *We* must turn from *our* wicked ways, then and only then has God promised to bring revival.

*　　*　　*

Charles Finney, a nineteenth-century evangelist, once told an audience of New York Christians:

> A holy church that would act on the principles of the gospel, would spread the gospel faster than all the money that ever was in New York, or that ever will be. Give me a holy church, that would live above the world, and the work of salvation would roll on faster than with all the money in Christendom.

Unfortunately, the church of Jesus Christ is so conformed to the world that except for a very few, we quite willingly ignore our assignment to teach the gospel and to make disciples of men—

to transform the world. Instead, we exchange spiritual substance for political activism, New Age doctrine, and material success.

Sadly, the farther away from Christ the church moves, the more judgmental we become of the lost. The more lax we become in our own faith, the more we expect the world to make up for our own shortcomings. Today, our churches don't even pray for revival.

Why?

Because quite frankly, it requires a level of seriousness and commitment that many of us don't want. So instead, we offer babes in Christ the milk of the Word, designed to keep our seats full—growing our numbers, expanding our tithe base, and building our buildings.

The result: We are conformed to this world and are ineffective as salt and light.

In Romans 12, Paul pleads with believers to *"be not conformed to this world: but be ye transformed"* (v. 2 KJV).

But what does that really mean? What is conformation? And what does it mean to be conformed to the world?

*   *   *

Merriam-Webster's Collegiate Dictionary defines *conformation* as acting *in accordance with prevailing standards or customs;*

... *To be similar or identical;*

... *To bring into harmony or accord* (10th ed., emphasis added).

Ask for your spiritual eyes to be opened and you should see some striking similarities between the world around you and any assembly line.

Every production line requires raw materials.

In life, you are the raw material.

In an automobile plant, blank metal and plastic are molded, shaped, stamped and assembled into a car.

The world has the same impact on us.

A production line has only one purpose. Without retooling, an automobile assembly lines cannot also produce computers.

Similarly, our assembly line [the world] has only one purpose—to keep us fixated on the world around us.

*   *   *

Because we are born from Adam, with a sinful nature, for most of us it takes very little effort to keep us on the assembly line. Even for those of us who have professed Christ.

Remember that God has given Satan temporary authority on earth, and Satan is the ultimate thief. He wants only to *"steal, and to kill, and to destroy"* (John 10:10). So naturally, Satan designed this world to be endlessly fascinating. His intent is to keep us in bondage from the day we're born until the day we die. He molds us, shapes us, and stamps us, all of which is designed to keep us focused on the temporal at the expense of the eternal.

For most of us, the pleasures of sin and the grind of our day-to-day struggles work together as one to keep us malleable and compliant. Dancing along like puppets, we are led down the primrose path, not to hell, but to an insignificant, meaningless life without substance or purpose.

Believers, we must know this, Satan will stop at absolutely nothing to keep us impotent and weak—and our flesh is his chief ally.

*   *   *

Think about this for a moment. Have you ever noticed the distractions that crop up whenever you are seeking after Christ? Or when you first got saved?

The distraction could be a better opportunity at work. Or maybe your child joins a new sports team that requires even more of your time. Or perhaps you lose your job. Or you develop a new relationship.

These distractions are subtle, nothing too out of the ordinary; they all seem so inevitable. And no, they're not necessarily bad things, but as distractions, they're effective. Why?

Because they keep our focus firmly fixed on the trivialities of everyday life at the expense of the revolutionary life that Christ wants us to live.

*　　*　　*

We must ask ourselves continually, "Are we conformed or are we transformed?"

I have found that there is one simple test.

Are you willing to share the gospel?

*　　*　　*

If you have to leave the country on a mission trip to share the gospel, then you're conformed.

If you can't remember the last time you shared Christ, then you're conformed.

If you've never shared the gospel with a coworker, then you're conformed.

If your neighbors have never heard that you are a follower of Christ, then you're conformed.

If your family doesn't know that you're saved, then yes, you're conformed.

*   *   *

Paul tells us that he is unashamed of the gospel of Christ.

> I am not ashamed of the gospel,
> because it is the power of God
> for the salvation of everyone who
> believes.

> ROMANS 1:16 NIV

To Timothy he says:

> Therefore do not be ashamed of
> the testimony of our Lord, nor
> of me His prisoner ... For this

reason I also suffer these things; nevertheless I am not ashamed, for I know whom I have believed and am persuaded that He is able to keep what I have committed to Him until that day.

II TIMOTHY 1:8, 12

Can we say the same?

*   *   *

Imagine living in a time or place where Christians face physical persecution. Imagine living in a country where coming to Christ could mean imprisonment or death.

It should come as no surprise that Christians living in countries where they suffer literal physical persecution have a completely different understanding of the Christian life. Because we here in the West hear so much about God's love, and so little of His judgment, we stand in awe of God's grace, and rightfully so. However, we have too little grasp of what is expected of us as believers—and the consequences of not fulfilling our obligations.

Yes, this watered-down version of our faith fills the pews and tickles itching ears, but it ignores the fact that there will ultimately come a day of judgment in which we will all stand before Christ to give an account of ourselves and our works, to see *"whether [they are] good or bad"* (II Corinthians 5:10).

Unfortunately, too many of us stop well short of any real commitment to Christ. We simply love the world too much. We are like Demas, of whom Paul wrote, *"[He] has forsaken me, having loved this present world"* (II Timothy 4:10).

*   *   *

But know this.

The sole purpose of Christianity is to produce men and women who are transformed by the revolutionary message of Jesus Christ.

And for those who have been transformed, our sole task is to

> Go ye therefore, and teach all nations, baptizing them in the name of the Father, and of the Son, and of the Holy Ghost: Teaching them to observe all things whatsoever I have commanded you.
>
> MATTHEW 28:19-20 KJV

That's it.

Yet in order to fulfill our purpose, we must understand that we are either conformed or being transformed.

There is no middle ground.

And if we are conformed and content, God's Word tells us that on the day of accountability, our Father will call us what we are—unworthy servants—unworthy of our calling, unworthy of God's grace.

Close your eyes for just a moment and iagine that you're stranded on an island.

What do you see? What are you thinking?

Are you thinking about food?

Water?

Shelter?

I'm not. And if you're honest, you're probably not either.

You're not thinking about any of that. Not yet, anyway. I mean, you will eventually, because your survival will ultimately depend on how quickly you can mentally and physically adapt to your new surroundings.

But still, right now, none of that has crossed your mind. Instead, if you're honest, your first thoughts are, "How do I get home?"

Just like Tom Hanks in *Cast Away*, no matter how long you're there or how comfortable you can make your "island paradise," you won't ever forget that this island is not really your home. You're never going to get so attached to it that you stop thinking about your real home, your family, your car, your clothes, or your dog.

It doesn't matter how long you're stranded on that island, you won't forget.

So what's the point?

We, the church of Jesus Christ, have forgotten that this world is not our home.

It feels real, doesn't it?

But all of this—our houses, our clothes, our work, our families—is only temporary. Fifty, sixty, seventy years maybe longer, but eventually, you're going home.

We are only pilgrims passing through to eternity, and when we stand before God on our judgment day, we should want to say with Paul:

> I have fought a good fight, I
> have finished my course, I have

kept the faith: Henceforth there is laid up for me a crown of righteousness, which the Lord, the righteous judge, shall give me at that day: and not to me only, but unto all them also that love his appearing.

II Timothy 4:7-8 KJV

S o how should we live?

We are commanded to be transformed.

Throughout Scripture, God gives us numerous examples of the transformed life and its impact.

Paul, formerly known as Saul, was admired for his zealous persecution of the believers. From Pharisee to chief among sinners, his transformation was radical and irrefutable.

Christ transformed Peter from an illiterate fisherman to a fisher of men to Cephas—the rock of the church. The change was so dramatic that when we read the account in Acts of Peter's explanation before the high priests Scripture says:

> When they saw the boldness of Peter and John, and perceived that they were unlearned and ignorant men, they marvelled; and they took knowledge of them, that they had been with Jesus.

ACTS 4:13 KJV

Zaccheus, a former tax collector, was called a traitor by his fellow Jews. But Jesus went to his house and transformed him from a man despised to a man respected for his integrity and generosity.

But perhaps, Moses is the most descriptive example of the transforming power of God.

In the Old Testament, we read that Moses asked God to "*show me Your glory*" (Exodus 33:18). The Lord responded by saying:

> You cannot see My face; for no man shall see Me, and live ... [but] here is a place by Me, and you shall stand on the rock. So it shall be, while My glory passes by, that I will put you in the cleft of the rock, and cover you with My hand while I pass by. Then I will take away My hand, and you shall see My back; but My face shall not be seen.

EXODUS 33:20-23

At the end of forty days and nights, Moses descended Mount Sinai. Exodus 34 tells us:

Moses did not know that the skin
of his face shone while he talked
with Him. So when Aaron and all
the children of Israel saw Moses,
behold, the skin of his face shone,
and they were afraid to come near
him.

EXODUS 34:29-30

*   *   *

The idea that we can and should walk so closely
with Christ that we begin to speak like Him; to
act like Him; to see others with His compassion;
and even begin to take on the physical reflection
of His glory. This is transformation.

L et's also agree on what transformation is not.

First, transformation is not automatic—it's not a given.

Just like the words of the old hymn, *"I have decided to follow Jesus, [with] no turning back,"* we too must decide to follow. Transformation requires a deliberate and daily decision to follow Christ.

*　　*　　*

Second, transformation is not free.

Salvation came at the expense of Christ's death and yes, is free to anyone who believes. But Jesus warned in Luke's Gospel that if we're actually going to follow Him, then we need to count the cost.

> And whoever does not bear his cross and come after Me cannot be My disciple. For which of you, intending to build a tower, does not sit down first and count the cost, whether he has enough to finish it—lest, after he has laid the foundation, and is not able

to finish, all who see it begin to
mock him."

LUKE 14:27-29

In other words, transformation will cost you.

*   *   *

Third, unlike salvation, transformation is not a
one-time event.

Most of us can remember where and when we
received Christ's salvation. But transformation
doesn't work like that. It's a process—one that
happens over the remainder of your life.

*   *   *

Lastly, although Paul tells us to work out our
salvation with "fear and trembling", we must
know that transformation is not self-induced.
Transformation is not some exercise in Spartan
willpower or behavior modification. Systematically
eradicating "bad" behavior from our lives does
not equal transformation. Simply trying on your

own to get rid of the weaknesses of your flesh will only lead to defeat and ultimately despair.

We must not forget that it is Christ who *"works in you both to will and to do for His good pleasure"* (Philippians 2:13).

*   *   *

Instead, we must see transformation as both a process and an end result.

The Christian life truly is a pilgrim's progress—a journey through which your mind, your will, your emotions, and your desires are realigned with the already finished work of Christ in your spirit.

But how does this happen?

If your spirit has already been transformed—and since you are unable to transform yourself—then what is your role in the process?

*   *   *

In the Psalms, King David cried out to God to

"create in me a clean heart" (Psalms 51:10 KJV), and so must we.

We cannot renew our hearts or our minds on our own; we can, however, allow God to create this in us. And once we surrender to Him to begin the process, we must cooperate until its completion.

So how do we stay in this place?

Humility and repentance.

*   *   *

Repentance is the key to transformation. It is how we keep open the lines of communication between us and God. Too many of us are afraid of this word. But we must understand that without repentance, there is no fellowship. Without repentance, there is no victory, and there is no growth.

But understand this, condemnation and guilt do not equal repentance. These are only the flawed substitutes offered by Satan.

Why?

Because he understands that just like Adam and Eve, guilt will make you run from the presence of God. Conviction and repentance, on the other hand, will bring freedom.

So how are we transformed?

The Holy Spirit convicts. You repent—agree with the conviction. You confess—verbal agreement—and accept Christ's forgiveness, knowing that *"He who has begun a good work in you will complete it until the day of Jesus Christ"* (Philippians 1:6).

Just as salvation is only the beginning of our journey in Christ, transformation does not end with repentance. Paul tells us that we must also renew our minds.

We wonder in amazement that we are so easily diverted by the things of the world and confused by false doctrines, when the only verse we know is John 3:16.

There is no substitute for knowing the Word of God. David says in Psalms 119: *"Thy word have I hid in my heart, that I might not sin against thee"* (v. 11 KJV). This is how the Holy Spirit works—through Scripture to give us revelation, inspiration, correction and instruction.

*　　*　　*

But perhaps, though, the most important reason that we should study and meditate on God's Word is to develop an accurate picture of Jesus Christ.

We are being transformed into His image, so we should want to know what that actually means.

Many of us have grown up with some ideas about Jesus. But just as many of us have found that the Jesus that we see in popular culture (and even much of today's popular theology) is very different from the Christ of the Scriptures.

In the Old Testament, God commanded the Israelites to keep His Word before their eyes always. Jesus Himself used Scripture to rebuke the devil, saying, *"It is written"* (Matthew 4:4).

The Berean believers were commended for their willingness to study the Word. They listened to what they heard from the apostles, but then searched the Scriptures themselves to see *"whether these things were so"* (Acts 17:11).

Just like the student who refuses to study and then is surprised when he or she receives a poor grade, know this: There is no power, there is no revelation, there is no truth, there is no victory, and there is no transformation apart from the Word of God.

It is the sword of truth.

*   *   *

But not only must you study; you must also learn to pray, to communicate with God.

Scripture teaches us that the *"effectual, fervent*

prayer of a righteous man avails much" (James 5:16) yet many of us don't pray, won't pray or have no idea how to pray. We either approach God carelessly or with no real belief in the power of prayer.

But prayer is powerful.

Elijah prayed that it wouldn't rain and it didn't for six months. He prayed again, and it started to rain.

*   *   *

In writing this, I am aware that it is very easy to become spiritually legalistic when we start to talk about any type of spiritual discipline.

So understand this. There is no magic number or phrase. There is no prescribed amount of time that we must spend with God each day. There is no prescribed posture—knees bent, head bowed, eyes closed. But we are told to pray without ceasing. So how do we do this?

I believe that we must mesh the two. Yes, you

need a time of concentrated communion with God, but you also need to begin to actively seek and practice the presence of God throughout your day. Rather than allowing our thoughts and our bodies to wander aimlessly through the day, we must learn to adopt an attitude of continual prayer which will lead us to closer communion with God and a stronger faith.

*   *   *

The third spiritual discipline that we must learn is fasting.

In Matthew 17, a man went to Jesus and asked him to cure his son, who suffered from severe epileptic seizures. When Jesus healed the boy, the disciples asked, *"Why could we not cast it out?"* (v. 19)

Jesus' response: *"This kind does not go out except by prayer and fasting"* (v. 21).

Nothing will strengthen the spirit and crucify the flesh like fasting. The result is that often we will hear what God is saying to us much more

clearly when we remove other distractions from
our lives.

*   *   *

The final key to transformation is worship.

Nehemiah 8:10 tells us that the *"joy of the Lord"*
will be our "strength." We see the truth of this in
the New Testament with Paul and Silas. Beaten
and thrown into prison for delivering a young girl
from an evil spirit, Acts says:

> At midnight Paul and Silas
> prayed, and sang praises unto
> God: and the prisoners heard
> them. And suddenly there was
> a great earthquake, so that the
> foundations of the prison were
> shaken: and immediately all the
> doors were opened, and every
> one's bands were loosed.
>
> ACTS 16:25-26 KJV

David dedicated the Psalms, an entire book of Scripture, to praising and worshipping God.

Having received the promise of Christ, how much more should we praise God?

Because of the cross, your debt is paid in full and you have eternal salvation.

Because of the cross, you are a new creation in Christ and can now stand boldly before Almighty God, your Abba Father.

Because of the cross, you are a joint heir with Christ.

Because of the cross, you have full access to the abundant life that Christ promised.

Because of the cross, you are filled with the power of the Holy Spirit.

No sacrifices. No priests.

Just you, standing clean and whole before Almighty God. Not because of anything that you have done, but because God loved us so much that He sent His Son, Jesus Christ, to die for us.

Does this sound too good to be true?

It isn't. There's no catch.

There is however, a condition.

*   *   *

Just as God, Our Father, presented His Son, Jesus, as the sacrifice for our sins, we too must present something: *"your bodies a living sacrifice"* (Romans 12:1).

Grace requires surrender.

It is not enough to be saved. We must surrender to the lordship of Jesus Christ. We must take up the cross, follow and obey. James 1 tells us that to hear the Word is not enough; we must also do what the Word commands.

*   *   *

Remember the story of Cain and Abel?

Cain, a farmer, offered to God part of his harvest—a sacrifice that was perfectly acceptable to him, but which came from his own pride, not from a willing and obedient heart.

The consequence?

God rejected Cain's sacrifice.

We must understand that God has very clear expectations of us, His children. Because of Jesus Christ, we are no longer required to bring animal sacrifices; however, we must still bring the "right" sacrifice. That is, we must offer ourselves.

Obedience is all that matters to God.

William Wilberforce was a 24-year-old member of the British House of Commons when he was called to follow Christ.

In the late eighteenth century, answering the call of God often meant entering the ministry or withdrawing from the world to live the monastic life. As a result, Wilberforce struggled for months to discover God's purpose for his life.

Should he renounce his promising career in politics to follow Christ?

For months, Wilberforce anguished over his decision. Fasting and praying, he sought God's heart and Godly counsel. John Newton, the former slave trader and a close family friend, advised him to keep his seat and look for ways to be used by God in Parliament.

Soon after, another close friend, William Pitt, the Prime Minister, wrote to him, "Surely the principles as well as the practice of Christianity are simple and lead not to meditation only, but to action."

For Wilberforce, this was confirmation. He kept his seat in Parliament.

One year later, God revealed to William His

purpose for his life. He wrote in 1787: *"God Almighty has set before me two great objects: the suppression of the slave trade and the Reformation of society."*

During the next two decades, Wilberforce led the abolition movement in England's Parliament. And each year for twenty years, every bill he authored to abolish the slave trade was defeated, until 1807, when Parliament finally voted to abolish slavery in England.

*   *   *

Sometimes we hear stories like this and we shake our heads in amazement at the power of God at work in someone else's life.

But these stories are not to be the spiritual exception. They are the rule.

A life that impacts the world for Christ is the natural result of our surrender to the will of God. It is the natural result of understanding that God's grace compels our submission and our obedience.

Wilberforce understood that he had been saved not only from something, but also to something. He did not wish to stand before Almighty God with empty hands, having failed to live up to the calling of Jesus Christ on his life—having failed to surrender.

He understood, as did Paul, that his profession of love for Christ could not be separated from his obedience. He understood that this was only his *"reasonable service"* (Romans 12:1).

*   *   *

Evidence of the surrendered life is summed up in the only two commandments that really matter: Love God and love your neighbor.

We've been reminded that our obedience is how we show God our love. So how do we love our neighbors? How do we prove to them God's perfect will?

First and most importantly, we must tell them about Jesus. Our inability—or our *unwillingness*—to share Christ wherever we go is proof, according to Scripture, that we are ashamed of Him, that we are conformed to this world, and that we do not love our neighbor.

Christ warns us about this:

> Whosoever therefore shall be ashamed of me and of my words in this adulterous and sinful generation; of him also shall the Son of man be ashamed.

Mark 8:38 KJV

*　　*　　*

Second, John tells us that the love of God not only means obedience, but also means action. If we can see someone in need and not offer him whatever we have, then we do not have the love of God, he says. So we must show love to our neighbors by being willing to sacrifice ourselves for them.

*　　*　　*

This of course, brings us back to the age-old question: Who is my neighbor?

Jesus answered this question for us with the parable of the Good Samaritan, but unfortunately, too many of us play mind games when answering this question.

We adopt some vague notion of "Christian-ish" behavior, and we're moved when we hear the latest missionary report at church. We bask in the reflected glory of those who have answered the all-consuming call of God for their own lives. We're the first to sign up for whatever mission trip is on offer, as long as it's far, far away and not on our own street.

We feel safe in our anonymous good deeds. They allow us to live lives that require little to no commitment and even less real sacrifice, especially for the people in our immediate vicinity.

But Romans 12:2 tells us that we must prove *"that good and acceptable and perfect will of God."*

Prove to whom? To the world.

Our willingness to live and give sacrificially is all the proof of Christ that the world is waiting for.

So how have we come to this place?

Quite simply, too many of us are not saved. Christ taught us the parable of the wheat among the tares; sadly, this is the picture of too many of our churches. Too many of us have made *decisions* about Christ, without ever really coming face to face with our sin and our true need for the Savior's mercy.

Paul wrote to the Corinthians, *"Godly sorrow worketh repentance to salvation not to be repented of"* (II Corinthians 7:10 KJV).

When people recognize themselves for what they really are—a sinner in the hand of an angry God—there is no decision. There is brokenness and sorrow. There is only repentance.

*   *   *

But what about those of us who are saved? What is our excuse?

We forgot.

We forgot that the substitution of Christ at Calvary was an exchange. Christ's physical death for our spiritual life. Our sins for the righteousness of Christ. His sacrifice for our service.

We forgot the elementary commands of our faith: *"Love the Lord your God with all your heart, with all your soul, with all your strength, and with all your mind, and your neighbor as yourself"* (Luke 10:27).

We forgot the revolutionary example of the early church and the awesome impact of a life lived through the power of the Holy Spirit.

We forgot that the true blessings of Christ—the peace that eclipses our understanding, the love of Christ, and joy in the Holy Spirit—come at a high cost indeed: our lives.

Instead, most of us refuse to take up Christ's yoke. We choose bondage over freedom. Until eventually, seduced by the desires and cares of this world, we give up. We shun the radical Christian life and are now content to merely go through the motions.

We try to have it both ways. We try to live a

sold—out life without really selling out. So we go to church and surround ourselves with believers. We worship with them, we eat with them, we hear the Word, and we substitute a pseudo-Christian environment for real, actual faith—forsaking our true calling for a pale and powerless substitute.

But know this, believer: There is no middle ground. If you are not being transformed, then you are conformed.

*   *   *

Too many times we've heard the story of the talents. So many times, in fact, that we delude ourselves into thinking that surely, God is talking to someone else.

Two servants were diligent. They used what had been entrusted to their care to increase the return on the master's investment. When the master returned from his journey, he said to each of them:

"Well done, good and faithful servant; you have been faithful over a few things, I will make you ruler over many things.

Enter into the joy of your lord."

MATTHEW 25:23

The third servant, like too many of us, was fearful, lazy, too self-involved to even take his master's money to the bank. Instead, he buried it in the ground. Read what the master said to this servant:

"Take the talent from him, and give it to him who has ten talents … and cast the unprofitable servant into the outer darkness. There will be weeping and gnashing of teeth."

MATTHEW 25:28; 30

Of course, we understand that the lesson is not in how many talents they were given, but in what they did with the talents that they received.

It is the same with you.

You have been called. You have been given talents, skills, and abilities.

Do you use them wisely—diligently investing in the eternal work of the kingdom? Understanding that there will come a day of accounting where you, like I, will stand before an Almighty God—the same God who would not let Moses see His face—and will answer for what you have done and not done.

Or have you buried your talents in the ground?

In the grand scheme of eternity, our lives here on earth are only a breath. There will be a day, and it is always sooner than we think, where you and I will stand before the judgment seat of Christ.

And we will stand there without excuse.

Do not ignore the master's utter lack of mercy when he dealt with his lazy and worthless servant.

Jesus told the church at Ephesus:

> "I have this against you, that you have left your first love. Remember therefore from where you have fallen; repent and do the first works, or else I will come to you quickly and remove your lampstand from its place—unless you repent."

REVELATION 2:4-5

The Word has not changed. For all of us who have forgotten, remember.

Remember and repent.

A Note To The Reader

This is not an easy book to read. It was even more difficult to write. However, it is my prayer that this book will point you to an ever closer relationship with Jesus Christ—a relationship that will transform your life and the lives of those around you.

Acknowledgements

Thank you Jim

Thank you Chandler

Thank you Mom and Dad

Notes

36 **one who shares Christ:** Merriam-Webster's Collegiate Dictionary, 10th ed., s.v. "evangelical."

41 **all the money in Christendom:** Charles Finney, "Lectures to Professing Christians" (New York: Smith & Valentine, 1836-37).

69 **must decide to follow:** "I Have Decided to Follow Jesus" [author unknown].

91 **the reformation of society:** For a detailed discussion of Wilberforce's spiritual awakening, see Eric Metaxas, Amazing Grace: William Wilberforce and the Heroic Campaign *to End Slavery* (Harper San Francisco, 2007).